We Celebrate

The Harvest

Bobbie Kalman

Susan Hughes

Janet Wilson **Greg Ruhl**

The Holidays & Festivals Series

Toronto New York Crabtree Publishing Company

The Holidays and Festivals Series
Created by Bobbie Kalman

For Joan

Writing team:
Bobbie Kalman
Susan Hughes

Illustrations:
Color illustrations by Janet Wilson
Black-and-white illustrations by Greg Ruhl
© Crabtree Publishing Company

Editor-in-Chief:
Bobbie Kalman

Editors:
Susan Hughes
Catherine Johnston
Maria Casas

Art direction and design:
Elaine Macpherson Enterprises Limited

Cataloguing in Publication Data
Kalman, Bobbie, 1947-
We celebrate the harvest

(The Holidays and festivals series)
Includes index.
ISBN 0-86505-044-9 (bound)
ISBN 0-86505-054-6 (pbk.)

1. Harvest festivals - Juvenile literature.
2. Thanksgiving Day - Juvenile literature.
I. Hughes, Susan, 1960- . II. Wilson, Janet
III. Ruhl, Greg IV. Title. V. Series.

GT4380.K34 1986 j394.2'683

350 Fifth Avenue
Suite 3308
New York, N.Y. 10118

102 Torbrick Road
Toronto, Ontario
Canada M4J 4Z5

Contents

Come celebrate the harvest

The boughs do shake and the bells do ring
So merrily comes our harvest in.
We have plowed and we have sowed,
We have reaped and we have mowed,
We have brought home every load.
Hip, hip, hurray for the harvest!

Come join the happy celebration. Children from all over the world are bringing gifts of the harvest. Can you see potatoes, red and green peppers, pumpkins, carrots, corn, okra, and tomatoes? Some children are carrying wheat, rice, rye, and baskets of fresh vegetables. Others are arriving with apples, papayas, plums, coconuts, pears, grapes, olives, and yams. Which of these are your favorite foods?

Dance and clap your hands to the music. Play games with your new friends. And now, before you begin your meal, join hands with the other children and sing a song of thanksgiving for the beautiful gifts of the harvest.

What is a harvest?

Everyone needs to eat, so people grow food. They grow wheat, apples, and grapes. They grow rice, sugar cane, and yams. They grow oranges, corn, and figs. They care for these crops for months. When a crop is ripe, people harvest it. This means they gather the crop and bring it in.

Foods are harvested at different times of the year in different parts of the world. In many places, the harvest is just before a cold or wet season. When the crop is harvested, both the crop and the time of harvesting it are called the harvest!

Thanks for the food

People work hard to grow and harvest crops, so they like to celebrate when the work is done. Harvest festivals are celebrated in almost every country of the world. They are celebrated at different times, in different ways, and are known by different names. However, the reason for harvest festivals is always the same — to give thanks for the food we eat.

Harvest festivals of long ago

Thousands of years ago, most people grew their own food. People believed that certain gods and goddesses helped the food grow. Each year at a special festival at harvest time, they thanked these gods and goddesses.

Honoring Demeter and Ceres

The early Greeks held a party for Demeter. Demeter was the Greek goddess who cared for fruits, vegetables, and grains. The Romans also had a goddess to whom they gave thanks. Her name was Ceres. She was the goddess of grain. A breakfast food was named after her. Do you know what it is? It's cereal!

At their harvest celebrations, both the Greeks and Romans played games. They enjoyed a huge feast at midnight. They roasted pigs and served the fruits and vegetables which had just been picked.

A parade for Min

The ancient Egyptians had a harvest parade in the spring. The Pharaoh or king was at the head of the parade, followed by crowds carrying grain and flowers. People brought these gifts to the temple of the harvest god, Min, in return for the food he helped them grow.

The Chinese Harvest Moon Festival

Hello to you, two-legged one! Do you know who I am? I am the Moon Rabbit. Have you ever heard of me? In China, I am quite a celebrity. That is because I have a special secret. I can make a potion from the leaves and bark of the cassia tree. One sip from the potion and you will live forever. No, I won't tell you how to make my potion, so don't ask. But I will promise you a long life if you are good!

The Moon Toad is also quite a celebrity. Is it because he has three legs? No. It is because he is a good friend of the Queen of the Sky. The Moon Toad promises wealth to those who try to please the Queen. That's why he's such a popular guy.

The Queen of the Sky

Who is the Queen? Look up in the sky tonight and you may see her. She is the moon!

Many people try to please the Queen, especially on her birthday. Her birthday is on the fifteenth day of the eighth full moon of the year. The eighth time that the Queen of the Sky circles the earth is one of her favorite times of the year. This is when people harvest their crops. Some people call the Queen "the harvest moon." They look up at her and say thank you for the harvest. She likes that.

On the Queen's birthday, people climb to their rooftops and hilltops to look for her. They say the moon is perfect on her birthday because she is full. They believe that the shape of a circle means happiness.

Round and round

How is the full harvest moon celebrated? Everyone eats round fruit and round cakes baked from the newly harvested wheat. They eat the round food on round plates.

The Moon Toad and I have a great time at this Moon Festival. We visit the earth, and people welcome us. They paint pictures of us on scrolls and hang them in their homes. Yes, we are real celebrities! When the festival is over, the scrolls are burned. Moon Toad and I ride the smoke all the way back to our home on the moon.

What a fun time of the year the harvest is! Don't you think this birthday party for the Queen is one of the best in the world, or even the universe? I do!

Celebrate the moon

Invite your friends to help you celebrate the Chinese Harvest Moon Festival. Tell them the story of the Moon Rabbit and the Moon Toad.

Make a Moon Rabbit

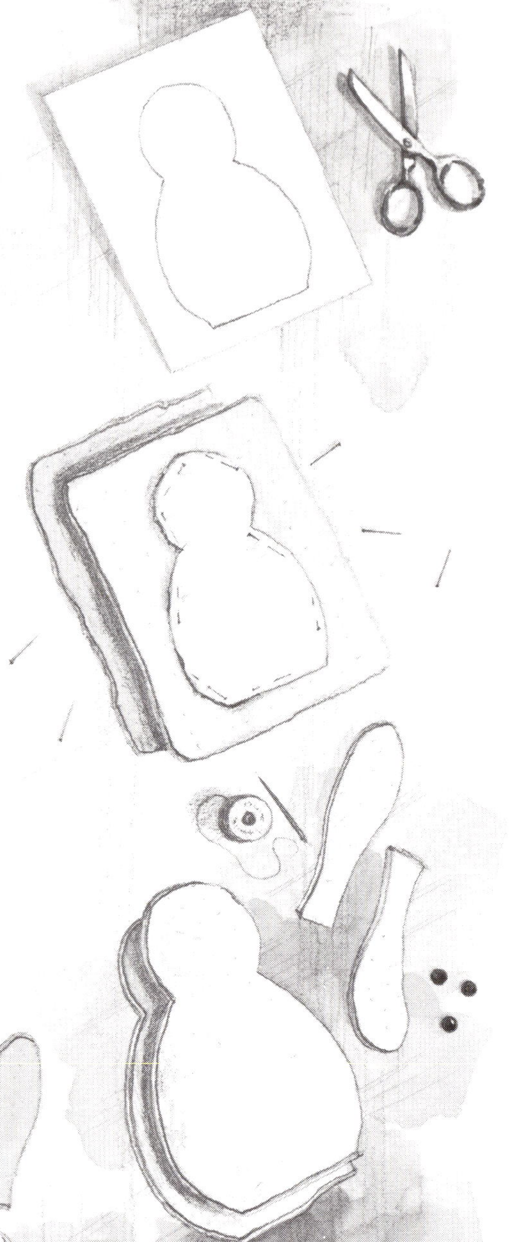

In China, children are given toy rabbits at the time of the Moon Festival. Make stuffed rabbits with your friends! To make one rabbit, you will need:

paper, pencil, scissors, pins
two pieces of felt and extra felt scraps
thread, large needle
cotton balls
sequins, glue

On a piece of paper, draw an outline of a rabbit. This will be your pattern. Cut out the pattern. Place the pieces of felt one on top of the other, and pin the pattern on top. Now cut the felt pieces into the shape of a rabbit by cutting around the rabbit pattern.

With a needle and thread, sew the two pieces of felt together along their edges. Leave one section open. Stuff the felt rabbit with cotton balls. Now sew up the opening. Glue on a sequin nose and sequin eyes. Cut extra felt scraps into ears and sew them on. Don't forget to glue on a cotton-ball tail. Your stuffed Moon Rabbit is now finished! If you like, use the same method to make a stuffed Moon Toad. Don't forget his third leg!

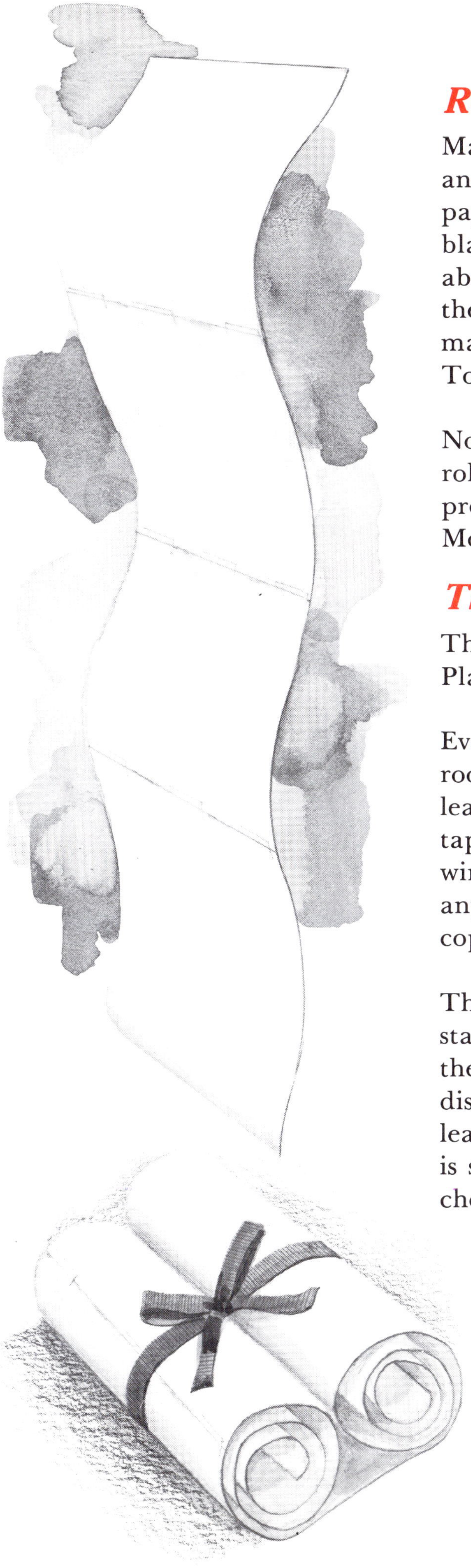

Roll a scroll

Make a scroll to welcome the Moon Rabbit and the Moon Toad. Make one long sheet of paper by taping together several sheets of blank white paper. Write a poem or story about the Rabbit and Toad, and print it on the scroll. Use paints, colored pencils, or felt markers to draw pictures of the Rabbit and Toad.

Now roll up the paper at each end until the rolls meet in the middle. Tie the scroll with a pretty red or green ribbon. On the day of the Moon Festival, unroll your scroll and display it!

The Circle Game

The circle means happiness to the Chinese. Play this game to celebrate the Moon Festival.

Everyone sits in a circle. One player leaves the room, and another player is chosen to be the leader. The leader begins a motion, such as tapping his or her feet, clapping hands, or winking. The leader can change the motion at any time and the other players must quickly copy it.

The player who has left the room returns and stands in the middle of the circle. By watching the changing motions, this player must try to discover which player is the leader. When the leader has been discovered, a different player is sent from the room and a new leader is chosen.

Sukkoth

Sukkoth is a Jewish harvest festival that lasts seven days in Israel and nine days outside Israel. It is also called the Feast of Booths. When the October festival draws near, Jewish families build *sukkoth* or booths in their gardens or on their porches. These booths are decorated with strings of berries and wreaths of flowers. Grapes, apples, other fruits, and stalks of wheat are hung on the inside walls. The roofs of the sukkoth are covered with evergreen branches.

The Jews build booths to remember a time, thousands of years ago, when the Jewish people wandered in the desert. Far from home, they lived in booths which they made of dry palms and branches. Then God led them back to their home in the land of Israel.

Special prayers

On every morning of Sukkoth except Saturday, many Jewish families eat their breakfasts in the booths. They thank God for having led them from the desert to their home in Israel. They also thank God for the harvest.

Each family member holds a *lulov* in one hand and an *ethrog* in the other hand. The lulov is a bundle of palm, willow, and myrtle leaves. An ethrog is a citron, which is a fruit like a lemon. The lulov and ethrog remind everyone of the good foods of the harvest.

Family members say a special blessing. They point in every direction to show that God is everywhere. On the eighth day of Sukkoth, they recite a thanksgiving prayer. They hope for a good harvest in the following year. On this last day, everyone sings and dances. Sukkoth is a happy time!

The day of Honensai

Today is the big day! Miki nervously rubs his sweating palms together. "Calm down, calm down," he tells himself. But he cannot. He has been looking forward to this day for many weeks now. Today is Honensai, the Japanese autumn festival. It is held to celebrate the rice harvest.

Miki is taking part in the festival tug-of-war for the first time this year. Only last week, he and his teammates carefully collected and dried rice stalks. Miki and his teammates twisted the rice stalks together to form a long, strong rope.

Some of the villagers used the leftover stalks to make little scarecrows. The older villagers call these scarecrows Ta-no-Kami, the name of the god of rice. They thank Ta-no-Kami for the good harvest and ask him to protect the next year's crop.

Miki saw several scarecrows in the rice fields this morning. He knows that some of the older villagers put them there because they believe the scarecrows will bring good luck to the crops. Most of the village families do not believe the old legends. Nevertheless, they make scarecrows because it is fun! Miki's little sister, Kaori, has been working on one for days now. Each time she finishes it, she decides it is not good enough and so she begins all over again! She wants to enter it in the "best scarecrow" contest.

Kaori wishes her brother luck. Miki stands with his teammates and tries to appear calm. It is difficult, especially when he sees his competitors and their supporters approaching from the nearby village. The air is full of shouts as the villagers greet one another with cries of "Good luck!" and "Maybe this year you will win!"

Miki takes his place behind Tanaka, and the other team members join the line. The opposing team lines up facing them. The teams grip the huge rope that Miki helped to make, and they wait nervously for the signal. Someone shouts, "Go!" The annual tug-of-war now begins.

Both teams are pulling with all their might. Miki leans back and digs in his heels. He uses muscles that he has been developing in the past weeks. All the team members are straining and gasping. Miki's team is winning! Now it is losing! Now it is winning again. The teams slowly pull each other forward and back, forward and back. Miki's body begins to ache. He hears Tanaka puffing.

The crowd shouts with excitement as first one team and then the other seems about to win. Miki is tiring. He wonders how much longer he can last. Then, suddenly . . .

What happened next?

Can you finish this story? Write your ending and then compare it with a friend's ending. The tug-of-war is an important contest in which these two villages in Japan take part during the Honensai festival. It is believed that the winning team will bring good luck to their village's rice crop in the following year!

Crop Over

Sugar cane is grown on the islands of the West Indies. Can you find the West Indies on a map? Barbados is one of these islands. It has a huge festival after the sugar-cane crop is harvested. This festival is called Crop Over.

A day of fun

A long time ago, the sugar cane was harvested by slaves on Barbados. The slaves had to work hard and were not treated well. For many weeks, they worked long hours cutting the sugar cane in the fields. When the last cane was cut, a worker rang the gong that hung in the yard. All the carts paraded in from the fields. The mules, oxen, and donkeys that pulled the carts were decorated with flowers. So were the carts and the people who rode in them! The endless work was finally over.

The next day was Crop Over. This was one of the few days of relaxation for the slaves who worked so hard during the harvest. Everyone danced and sang all day and night.

Contests, contests, contests

Crop Over is still celebrated in Barbados when the harvesting of the sugar cane is finished. The difference today is that there are no slaves. This is another reason for celebrating!

Crop Over lasts for three weeks. People dress up in crazy or beautiful costumes. There are contests to pick the best musical bands. There are contests to see who can cut sugar cane the fastest and who can drink the most coconut milk! A Crop Over Queen is chosen to lead the festivities.

Good-bye Mr. Harding

On the last day of the celebrations, a bonfire is lit. On it is placed an old sack of sugar cane dressed in a black coat and top hat. This figure is called Mr. Harding. Mr. Harding reminds people of the hard times. When Mr. Harding is burned, everyone says good-bye to the hard times. They celebrate freedom. They celebrate the days of rest after the hard work of harvesting is over.

Pongal, a rice harvest in India

In southern India, there are usually two rice harvests each year. One harvest is in January. People celebrate this harvest for three days with a celebration called Pongal. For many days, families prepare for Pongal. They paint their homes. They paint designs on walls or draw rice-flour designs on the floors. Everyone buys new clothes.

A thanksgiving

The first day of the festival arrives. Everyone goes to the temple to thank the gods for the rains that have made the harvest a good one. They give thanksgiving gifts to the gods. These gifts include large clay horses which are lined up outside the temple.

On the second day of the festival, the women rise early and bathe in a nearby stream or the temple pool. Then they hurry home to begin cooking the rice which has been harvested. Some people believe that if the rice boils quickly, the year will be a good one!

Pongal! Pongal!

As soon as the rice begins to boil, the women call out, "Pongal! Pongal!" *Pongal* means "to boil." That is why Pongal is the name of this rice-harvest celebration. Pongal is also the name of the sweets that the women are making. They mix the cooked rice with sugar, fruits, butter, and oil. Some of the pongal is offered to the gods, and then the family enjoys the tasty sweets.

Thanking the cows

The third day of Pongal honors the cows. Many people in India believe that cows are special because they provide people with milk, which is an important food. The cows are washed and their horns are painted in bright colors. Garlands of fruit and flowers are put around their necks. Sometimes the cows are even allowed to taste the pongal that is left over!

Festa dos Tabuleiros

Welcome to my home! I live in a town called Tomar in the country of Portugal. You have come to visit me at a very special time. We are about to celebrate a harvest festival. We only celebrate this festival once every three years because it is very expensive. We have been saving our money so we can have a grand celebration!

Our festival is called the Festa dos Tabuleiros. Can you speak Portuguese? If you can, you know that *festa* is the Portuguese word for festival. *Tabuleiros* is the Portuguese word for trays. In English, our harvest festival is called the Festival of Trays. Let me explain why we call it by this name.

Tall hats

The trays are really giant hats that we have made. We cover them in layers of bread and flowers. The bread comes from wheat, one of the gifts of the harvest. My girlfriends and I wear long, white dresses for the festival. We put on our tall hats and parade through the town.

Sounds of the parade

The priests walk behind us. They carry black pillows with silver crowns on them. Can you hear the brass band that follows the priests? Now listen again. Do you hear mooing? The cows are at the end of the parade. They have flowers on their heads and horns. What a pretty procession!

Sharing the harvest feast

Now join us for a feast! Everyone is welcome. We will eat fresh bread and roasted meat. After we have eaten as much as we can, the leftover meat and bread will be auctioned off. The money raised by the auction is given to those in our village who need it. Don't you think this is a perfect way to end our festival of thanksgiving?

Harvest words

Try to use all these words in your own harvest story.

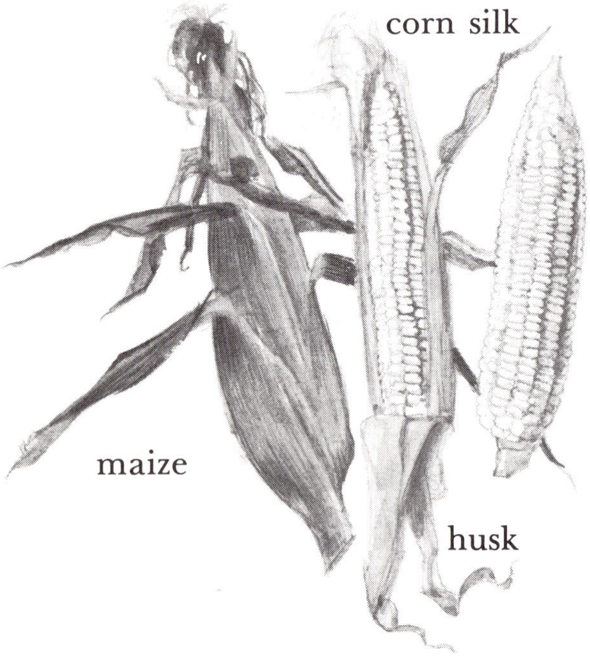

yam

pumpkin

pumpkin pie

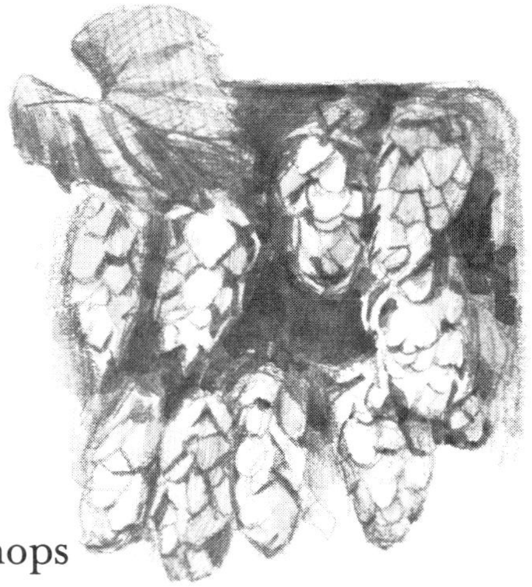

hops

turkey

bonfire

papaya

coconut

sugar
cane

cornucopia

plantain

Celebrating the corn

Travel back to the days of long ago in North America. Can you see the Indians of the Eastern Woodlands harvesting corn? This is a special kind of corn called maize. Listen to the women sing as they remove the husks. One of them finds a colored ear of corn. This means she may keep two extra corncobs for herself! Maybe she will hang them as a decoration in her longhouse.

After the work is done, join the Indians at a wonderful party. Feast on geese, ducks, wild turkey, and deer meat, which is called venison. Play games of skill. Can you keep a ball in the air by using only your hands?

In the evening, sit with the others around a huge bonfire and roast corn. Does the bonfire remind you of the sun? Without the sun, nothing would grow. Watch as the Indians perform special dances as a part of this harvest festival. They are thanking their gods for the sun and moon, rivers and streams, wind and rain, and all the other gifts of nature.

Have a "corny" time

Corn was one of the most important crops for the Indians and early settlers. Try these "corny" activities and recipes. Have a parent, older brother or sister, or your teacher help you use the stove, oven, or barbecue.

Corn decorations

Indian corn makes a beautiful harvest decoration. Peel down the husks of two or three ears of corn so that the colorful corn kernels show. Remove the hair-like corn silk. Tie the corn husks together at the base with an orange, yellow, or brown ribbon. Hang your corn bouquet on your front door, on the wall, or over a fireplace.

Roasted corn

The Indians and settlers used to roast corn. If you have a barbecue, you can roast corn, too! Remove the thick outer husks of several ears of corn. Peel back, but do not remove, the inner husks. Remove the corn silk. Spread soft butter on the kernels and then replace the husks over the corn. Place the ears of corn on a barbecue for twenty to thirty minutes, turning them every few minutes. When they are done, you have a hot, buttered treat!

Cornbread

Cornbread is easy to make and tastes delicious when it is fresh.

You need:

250 mL (1 cup) cornmeal
250 mL (1 cup) flour
60 mL (¼ cup) melted butter
1 egg
60 mL (¼ cup) brown sugar
60 mL (¼ cup) molasses
250 mL (1 cup) milk
15 mL (1 tablespoon) baking soda
5 mL (1 teaspoon) ginger

Preheat oven to 215°C (425°F). Mix ingredients together and pour into greased, square cake pan. Bake 20-30 minutes. The cake is done when a knife stuck in the center comes out clean.

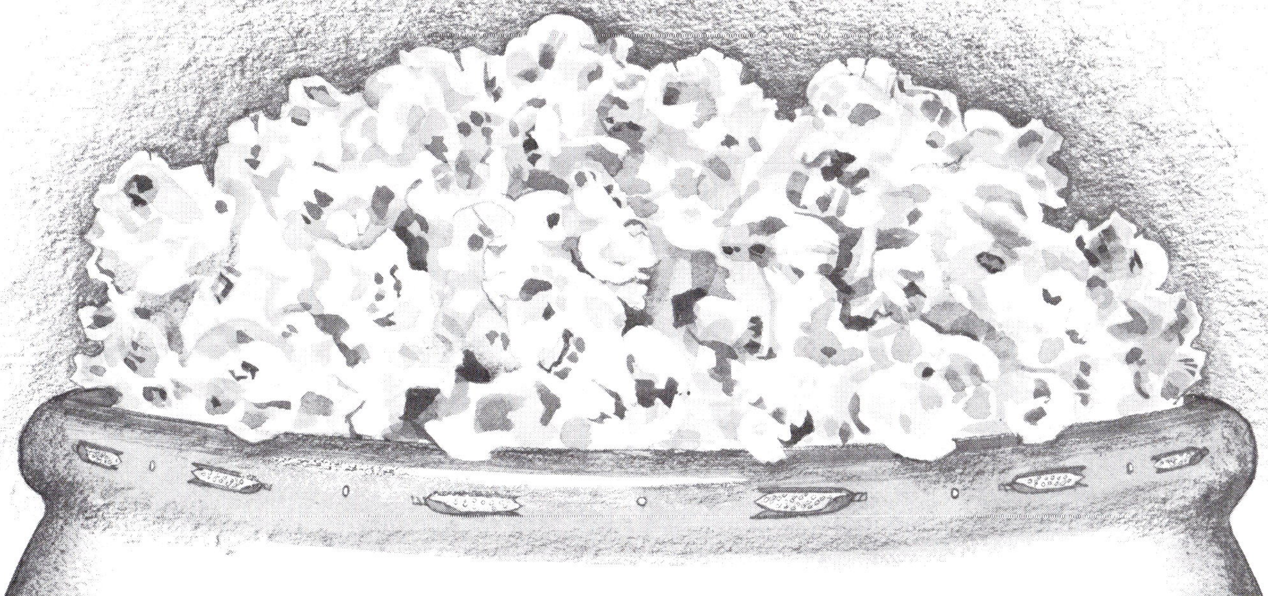

Pop! Pop! Pop!

The Indians taught the early settlers how to make popcorn. They popped corn in clay jars and then poured maple syrup over it. The settler children loved this snack. Since then, people have put all kinds of toppings on popcorn.

Terrific toppings

Try some of these toppings on freshly popped corn.

Shake it on!

Pour melted butter over popcorn. Shake any or all of these on your buttered corn: parmesan cheese, sesame seeds, garlic salt, seasoned salt, or cinnamon sugar.

Maple butter Melt 15 mL (1 tablespoon) of butter and add 60 mL (¼ cup) of pure maple syrup.

Peanutty honey Melt some peanut butter and add a touch of honey.

Cheesy corn In a saucepan, melt some cheese spread over low heat and pour over popcorn. Sprinkle chili powder on top for added zing!

Harvest Home

The festival of Harvest Home has been celebrated for hundreds of years in England. Long ago, people worked hard in the fields each autumn cutting the stalks of wheat, barley, and rye, and bundling them together. The harvesters cheered when the last of the grain was loaded onto a wagon. The final sheaf of grain was special. So was the person who cut it! This lucky person, called the Lord of the Harvest, rode back from the fields on top of the swaying wagonload. The rest of the villagers sang and laughed. They raced alongside the wagon, urging the horses on.

All the harvesters ended the day at a big table piled high with food. They gave thanks for their supper and for the grain harvest. Then the hungry workers attacked their food with great gusto!

Decorating the churches

At Harvest Home, people decorated the churches all over the countryside. They hung up sheaves of golden grain tied with ribbons. They displayed the fruits and vegetables that had been harvested from the gardens. Bright red apples and tomatoes, orange pumpkins and squash, and green peppers and beans added a burst of color to the special harvest services at the church.

The newly harvested wheat was ground into flour and then baked into a special loaf of bread. This loaf was put on the altar of the church. When the church service was over, the food that had been used to decorate the church was given to needy people so that everyone could enjoy the gifts of the harvest.

Today, many people in England still decorate their churches with flowers and food during Harvest Home.

Your own harvest festival

Invite some friends over to have some harvest fun with you, or persuade your teacher to have a harvest festival in your classroom.

A centerpiece of fall colors

Bring the beautiful colors of fall into your living room or classroom by making a Thanksgiving centerpiece. Cut a round hole in the top of a medium-sized pumpkin. Scoop out the seeds and the mushy insides. Fill a plastic container with sand and place the container in the pumpkin. Find branches of colorful fall leaves and push the ends firmly into the sand.

A leafy window

Save the beautiful colors of autumn! Using red, orange, green, and yellow leaves, make a leafy window that looks like stained glass.

Lay a piece of newspaper on an ironing board. Place a sheet of waxed paper on top of the newspaper. On this piece of waxed paper, arrange your leaves in a pretty design.

Now, place a second sheet of waxed paper and another piece of newspaper on top of the leaves. Ask a parent, teacher, or older brother or sister to iron the newspaper until the waxed papers underneath have started to melt. The two layers will stick together with your leaf pattern held in between. Discard the newspapers. Let your colorful leafy window cool for five minutes. Then hang it up for everyone to see!

A cardboard cornucopia

Do you know what a cornucopia is? It is a horn-shaped container overflowing with harvest foods. Cornucopia means "horn of plenty." It is a symbol of a good harvest.

You can make a horn of plenty. Cut a large triangle-shaped horn from a piece of construction paper. Paste this horn on a sheet of bristol board. Cut fruits and vegetables, such as red apples, purple grapes, yellow bananas, orange carrots, green peppers, and yellow ears of corn, from colored construction paper. Glue the fruits and vegetables onto the board so that they seem to overflow from the horn.

A patchwork wallhanging

Cut out sixteen to twenty square fabric patches in different colors. On a piece of paper, draw a harvest picture, such as an ear of corn, colorful leaves, a wagon full of hay, or a scarecrow! Cut out the picture. Place it on a piece of colorful material and cut around it. Now glue or sew the piece of material onto one of the fabric squares. Decorate the material. Have each of your friends design one or two squares. Then sew them together to form a wallhanging. Hang your harvest work of art on a bulletin board or wall.

Kick up your heels!

Find a square-dance record in your library. Listen to the instructions being called out while the music plays. Practice with your friends. If you are still having problems, turn the page and learn how to square-dance from these experts. Hope your harvest party is as much fun as theirs!

Swing your partner!

Harvest facts

Did you know that people in Greece harvest olives from olive trees? When the olives are ripe, people go to the olive groves and beat the tree branches with sticks. The olives fall to the ground and are collected in baskets. Raw olives are hard and bitter, so they are pickled before they are eaten. This makes them taste good!

Did you know that in some countries such as Germany and Switzerland, the cattle are brought down from the mountain pastures in the autumn? This is a time of celebration. The cattle are decorated with feathers, red ribbons, and flowers carved from wood. They wear bells around their necks. Sometimes the cow that leads the herd wears a crown made of little pieces of painted wood. Attached to its crown is a tiny, decorated fir tree.

The villagers play music and ring bells to welcome the animals and the herdsmen who have cared for the cattle during the summer. Now the cattle will be kept in the village barns during the cold winter months.

Did you know that in Poland, people have a special tradition when they finish harvesting the wheat? The last woman cutting grain is wrapped up in the last sheaf of wheat. People call her Baba or Old Woman. She is sprinkled with water to make sure that the rain will come again for next year's crop.

In Bulgaria, there is a similar custom. The last sheaf of grain is called the Corn Queen. The villagers dress this sheaf in women's clothing and carry it through the village streets. Then the Corn Queen is thrown into the well or the river so there will be rain for the next year's harvest.

Did you know that more than 170 years ago Oktoberfest was a wedding celebration? It took place in Munich, Germany, and everyone had so much fun that the King decided there should be a big party at the same time every year! In later days, Oktoberfest became a celebration of the hop harvest. Hops are the dried, ripe flowers of the hop plant which are used to make beer.

Oktoberfest means October fair. Today, it is a huge festival. More than two million people visit Munich during the two weeks of celebration. They dance and sing. They drink beer, join arms, and sway from side to side. There are also big Oktoberfest events in areas of Canada and the United States where many people of German background live.

Did you know that in some German towns there is a three-day festival to honor the patron of herdsmen, Saint Bartholomew? People celebrate with sports, contests, costumes, and a parade. The highlight of the festival is the Shepherd's Race. Shepherds and shepherdesses race in pairs across a field. They have bare feet! The winners are congratulated at the Shepherd's Dance that night.

Did you know that in Greece there is a spring harvest festival of fish? It takes place in a small town called Megara. Fish are an important "crop" in this town. Dancers at the festival imitate the movements of the fishermen pulling in the heavy nets full of fish.

Did you know that in Italy the harvest celebration is called Ferragosto? Ferragosto means August fair. People wearing papier-mâché masks and costumes dance through the streets. There are fireworks and music. Everyone takes the day off work to celebrate the harvest!

Thanksgiving — a family day

In the United States and Canada, the harvest festival is called Thanksgiving. Thanksgiving is a family day. Family members often travel great distances to be with one another. Together they enjoy big dinners which include turkey, cranberry sauce, and pumpkin pie. For most Canadians and Americans, the most important part of this holiday is giving thanks for family, friends, food, and all the good things that have happened in the past year.

The story of the Pilgrims

Thanksgiving got its name from a harvest celebration that took place over 350 years ago. In 1620, a group of people we call the Pilgrims set out on a voyage across the ocean. They sailed from England to Plymouth, Massachussets on a ship called the Mayflower. It was a difficult trip. When they landed, things were not much easier. It was the beginning of a cold winter. The Pilgrims found it hard to stay warm in the simple homes they had built. There was not enough food to keep people healthy, and many of them died.

When spring came, things were a little better. The Pilgrims were very happy to make two good Indian friends, Samoset and Squanto. Squanto became the guide and teacher of the Pilgrims. He and Samoset showed the Pilgrims how to dry fruit and plant corn. They helped them to hunt animals, catch fish, and dig for clams. Samoset introduced the Pilgrims to Chief Massasoit and the Wampanoag Indians who lived nearby. The Pilgrims and Indians became good friends and agreed always to help one another.

A day of thanksgiving

When the beginning of October came, the settlers had a harvest to be proud of! This was the time of year that they had always celebrated Harvest Home in England. Governor Bradford, the leader of the Pilgrims, decided that the first harvest in the New World should be an especially big celebration. He invited Chief Massasoit and his people to a big feast. The celebration was called "a day of thanksgiving."

The Pilgrims went hunting and fishing. They picked fruit and baked bread. Chief Massasoit and the Indians arrived with five deer to add to the feast. Because there were so many people, the celebrations were held outside. Long tables were made by placing planks of wood on top of sawhorses.

Preparing the feast

The feast was huge! Meat was roasted over big, open fires. There was venison (deer meat), wild turkey, geese, clams, eels, cornbread, and fish. The guests enjoyed gooseberries, strawberries, cherries, and plums.

For the children, the most exciting part of the feast came when the Indians heated corn over the fire in earthen jars. The kernels burst into white puffs! Maple syrup was poured over the freshly popped corn. What a delicious treat!

An official Thanksgiving

People continued to celebrate the harvest and give thanks for the new land in the years following this first American Thanksgiving. People around the country celebrated Thanksgiving on different days. Then, in the 1800s, many people wanted the whole country to celebrate on the same day. In 1863, President Lincoln chose the last Thursday in November as the national Thanksgiving Day. Ever since then, this day has been Thanksgiving Day in the United States.

Sarah's first Thanksgiving

Sarah searched high and low for the blackberry bushes. She knew they were somewhere in this corner of the woods, perhaps just a bit further. Well, maybe over by the stream. No, they were not there either. Suddenly, Sarah stopped. She was lost!

In a panic, she ran towards a patch of sunlight. In the rush of tumbling skirts and whipping branches, she lost her basket. Then she tripped over a root and sprawled flat on her stomach.

Sarah thought of her mother waiting at home for the berries. She had been so excited about baking her first Thanksgiving pie, and now Sarah would be letting her down! Her mother was cooking a splendid Thanksgiving dinner, just like the Harvest Home feasts they had always enjoyed back in England. Her father had bagged his very first wild turkey last night. The berries would have been Sarah's contribution to the dinner.

Suddenly, Sarah noticed a delicious smell in the air. She slowly opened her eyes. She had fallen right into a blackberry bush! Then, a twig snapped, sounding like a gunshot in the silent woods. Sarah's head jerked up. She gasped. Standing before her was a young Indian boy. He came closer, knelt by Sarah, and showed her a berry. He seemed to be saying, "Do you want this?" Sarah stared at him. Then she held out her apron in reply.

Together, she and her new friend picked enough berries for three Thanksgiving pies! When Sarah's apron was filled to overflowing, the boy stood up and beckoned. Sarah followed. In less than ten minutes, they had arrived at the clearing where Sarah's house stood.

That evening, the family gave thanks for their harvest, their new home, and for the friends who had helped them in the first difficult year. They also gave thanks for Sarah's new friend, who had brought their daughter back, and who was now on his third piece of blackberry pie!

Giving thanks

When we give thanks, we sometimes look into the past. We remember happy times and special occasions. We also give thanks for what we now have and hope for good things to come.

In your mind, collect short scenes of people and events that have made you happy in the past, and think of some events that might make you happy in the future. Watch your "mind movie" every once in a while and review all those things you are thankful for.

Let's share!

Sit in a circle with a group of friends. Think of one thing that has happened to you in the past year that you are truly thankful for. Tell it to your friends. Ask one of your friends to retell your experience and then share an experience for which he is thankful. Then a second friend must retell your experience and the first friend's experience before she tells what she is thankful for. Continue around the circle. In this way, everyone in the circle enjoys the happiness of everyone else.

For all these things

For flowers that bloom about our feet,
For tender grass so fresh and sweet,
For song of bird and hum of bee,
For all in nature we hear or see,
We give thanks.

For white of cloud and blue of sky,
For pleasant shade of branches high,
For fragrant air and cooling breeze,
For beauty of the blooming trees,
We give thanks.

For this new morning with its light,
For rest and shelter of the night,
For everything the good earth lends,
For health and food, for love and friends,
We give thanks.

Canadian Thanksgiving

Many of the voyagers who first sailed to Canada held thanksgiving celebrations. A group of English explorers led by Sir Martin Frobisher arrived in Newfoundland in 1578. They gave thanks for their safe arrival in the New World after a long, dangerous sea journey. Other early settlers also celebrated safe arrivals and, in later years, set aside special days when they gave thanks for their new homes and successful harvests!

The Order of Good Cheer

Over three hundred years ago, Samuel de Champlain and a group of French settlers landed in what is now Nova Scotia. They had a difficult winter of hunger and sickness, but in the spring, the courageous settlers planted crops such as rye, hemp, wheat, barley, and oats. That autumn, there was plenty for everyone to eat.

Champlain formed a club to celebrate the harvest. The club was named the Order of Good Cheer. The settlers took turns making huge dinners and entertaining one another. They spent happy evenings talking, singing, and feasting around a warm fire. They shared their thanksgiving suppers and good cheer with their friendly Indian neighbors. They gave thanks to God for a new beginning in a new land.

Many ways of celebrating

More and more settlers arrived in Canada to begin new lives. They all had special ways of giving thanks for their harvests. Many of them were English. They celebrated using some of the Harvest Home traditions, just as the Pilgrims had. Irish, Scottish, French, German, Ukrainian, Jewish, and other European settlers also added their own traditions to the Canadian harvest celebrations. Many Loyalist Americans moved to Canada after the American Revolution and continued to celebrate Thanksgiving every year. The customs of all these settlers helped to make the Canadian Thanksgiving celebration what it is today!

Getting together

For many years, no special date was set aside for Thanksgiving. At first, it was celebrated on November 6. Then Thanksgiving Day was changed to the second Monday in October. This day is now a holiday for everyone in Canada.

Most Canadians spend Thanksgiving Day with their families. They may go for a drive through the countryside to admire the beautiful colors of the autumn leaves. The air is cool, but the sun is bright. A big turkey dinner followed by hot pumpkin pie with whipped cream on top is the highlight of the celebration!

The trouble with Tillie Turkey

Tillie was Tom Mitchell's turkey. Tom's father had brought her home one day when she was just a tiny bird. She wasn't the type of pet anyone would cuddle up with. She wasn't cute. In fact, Tillie was kind of ugly. Tom didn't care, though. He loved Tillie.

Tom had chores to do before and after school each day. He chopped wood for the stove. He milked Bonnie, the cow, and collected the eggs the hens had laid. Tillie followed Tom as he did his chores.

She pecked at his heels and talked to him in turkey language. "Gobble, gobble, gobble," she said all day long. Tillie was a talkative turkey! Tom understood what she meant, though. She asked how his day had been. She reminded him when it was time to milk Bonnie.

Tillie even perched on the back of Tom's chair while he did his homework. Tom told his mother that Tillie knew all the answers to his arithmetic problems. Tom's mother was doubtful. All she could hear was, "Gobble, gobble, gobble."

Tom's parents did not want him to become too fond of Tillie. Each year, the Mitchells had a big turkey dinner for Thanksgiving. Tom's father had bought Tillie to be fattened up for Thanksgiving dinner. Now, it was the day before Thanksgiving.

Mr. Mitchell decided to talk to Tom about Tillie. "You know, Tom, your mother is thinking of trying a new chestnut dressing in the turkey for Thanksgiving tomorrow," he began nervously. Tillie started to gobble angrily, as if she had understood every word.

"You can't be planning to eat Tillie, Dad!" Tom exclaimed. "I won't *let* you hurt Tillie. I'd rather starve!" Tom jumped up and left the porch with Tillie, as usual, following closely at his heels.

Just before dawn the next morning, Mr. Mitchell woke up, got dressed, and went to the barn. Tillie was alone. She stood there and looked him straight in the eye. Tom's father knew then what he had to do.

Mr. Mitchell returned to the house just as Tom and his mother were eating breakfast. "We're having Tillie for dinner tonight," he announced. Tom burst into tears and ran out to the barn. He threw himself onto a haystack and sobbed and sobbed.

Just then, he felt a familiar pecking on the back of his neck. He heard, "Gobble, gobble, gobble." He turned to look. Tom couldn't believe his ears or eyes. There stood Tillie! Tom's parents entered the barn. Tom began to smile as his father explained that Tillie was coming to Thanksgiving dinner, not as the meal — but as a guest!

It was the most wonderful Thanksgiving ever. Tom and his parents enjoyed a delicious meal of fish, freshly baked bread, vegetables, and apple pie. Tillie sat perched at her favorite spot on Tom's chair. And when the family gave thanks for their food and for one another, Tillie joined in with a "gobble, gobble, gobble!" What do you think she was really saying?

The harvest beat

Reach up high, stand on your toes,
Pluck the fruit which on the branch grows.
Reach for the apple, reach for the pear,
Over here and over there.

Now bend down and look around,
Gather vegetables from the ground.
Pull the carrots, bend your knees,
Pluck tomatoes, beans, and peas.

Pick the grapes which grow on the vine,
Plump and juicy with sunshine.
Drop them in the bucket, stamp your feet,
Make grape juice with the harvest beat!

Do a somersault frontwards and back,
Lift that bail and carry that sack.
Swing that scythe from side to side,
Bounce up and down on the haywagon ride.

Stretch to your left, stretch to your right.
Harvest this food in the autumn sunlight.
Twist and turn, kick up your heels,
Clap your hands and dance the reels!

Harvest recipes

These children from around the world are cooking up a storm. The recipes they are using are made from the fruits and vegetables of the harvest. Try some of these recipes with your family or older friends. You may want to make them a part of your harvest-celebration dinner this year.

Rice is nice

Rice is a staple food for many people. That means it is an important part of their diet. Many people in Japan, China, and India eat rice every day. How often do you eat rice? Make it tonight using this recipe.

A ring of rice

500 mL (2 cups) long-grain rice
80 mL (⅓ cup) French salad dressing
60 mL (¼ cup) chopped green pepper
60 mL (¼ cup) chopped red pepper
2 stalks celery, thinly sliced
4 chopped green onions
6 pitted black olives

Cook rice, following directions on box. Pour dressing over hot rice and mix well. Add other ingredients (except olives) and mix well. Brush the inside of a ring mold with oil. Spoon in rice mixture and pat it down firmly. Put in refrigerator for 3 hours. Turn rice out of mold on flat plate and place olives on top.

A festival of yams

In West Africa, one of the most important crops is the yam crop. A yam is a vegetable similar to a sweet potato. In Ghana, West Africa, there is a yam festival each year. Everyone dresses in fancy clothes. They parade through the streets to the sound of drums and flutes. Then everyone feasts on roasted yams, fish, and nuts.

Candied Yams

6 medium yams
125 mL (½ cup) brown sugar
45 mL (3 tablespoons) butter or margarine
45 mL (3 tablespoons) cream or milk

Boil yams with skins on. Remove skins when yams are cooked. Cut yams into slices. Combine other ingredients together in a saucepan and cook over low heat. Add yam slices and stir gently until each one is coated with the sweet sauce. Serve hot.

Especially for Thanksgiving

Apples and cranberries are an important part of Thanksgiving dinner. Combine both in this easy dessert recipe.

Cranberry apples

60 mL (¼ cup) butter or margarine
60 mL (¼ cup) sugar
250 mL (1 cup) frozen or canned cranberries
8 apples with cores removed

Combine butter or margarine, sugar, and cranberries. Place cored apples on pieces of buttered aluminum foil. Stuff with cranberry mixture. Close foil around each apple and bake in oven for 20 minutes at 180°C (350°F).

Kalunga!

Once upon a time on a far-away planet called Bloop, two creatures were trying to solve a problem.

"We give the Sprackets food every year," Gloop, a turquoise Skittle, said to Freep. "And it's good food too — rachews, nonnets, and even freens! But every peon they need more."

Freep, who was large and hairy, agreed. "I know, Gloop. You're right. This has gone on for peons and peons. They just don't seem to be able to grow enough. But believe me, they don't like asking us for food."

"Oh, of course they don't," said Gloop quickly, as he gallumphed back and forth across the floor, "but there must be a better way. One day, we may not have extra food. Then what will happen? The Sprackets will all go hungry!"

The two creatures looked at one another. Freep wrung her hands in distress as she tried to think of a solution.

Suddenly, there was a clacket at the door. "Come in," called Gloop. In walked a tall Spracket called Martle.

"Ah, yes," Gloop said, smiling. "I guess you've come about the food. We'll be getting it for you immediately."

"Actually," said Martle, "I was wondering if we might think of a better solution to our food problem. It's quirtle of you to give us food every peon, but it doesn't seem to be a very practical solution."

"Indeed, indeed," caddled Freep. "Do you have any ideas, Martle?"

"Actually," said Martle with a wink of her big orange eye, "I have a solution."

"What is it? What is it?" Freep spurgled, her spots turning from purple to pink.

"You know how to grow food, right? You're good at growing food. Well, what if, instead of giving us food, you teach *us* how to do a better job of growing it?" said Martle.

"What a moorvy idea!" Freep cried. "It's the perfect answer. We know a lot about growing food. Together, we can work on improving your food-growing methods. Soon you'll be growing as much food as we are! You'll be self-sufficient."

"And if we ever need food," Gloop chortled, "you can help us!" Gloop's eyes opened wide and his ears twitched. "Kalunga!" he cried happily. "We'll all be better off!"

"Kalunga!" Gloop, Freep, and Martle all skawaggled. They hugged one another. "That was such a simple solution," marveled Gloop and Freep. "Why didn't *we* think of it?"

Martle winked at them with her other big orange eye.

Plenty for everyone

Please join our picnic. Come dance and sing!
Add your food to what others bring.

Let's all join hands and shout, "Hurray!"
It's time to celebrate in a brand-new way.

The harvest is here and we want to share
Our food with people everywhere.

We'll wipe out hunger if we all give
The knowledge we have to help others live.

Each one of us has the right to eat.
Why don't we all work until hunger is beat?

We can learn new methods of growing crops.
If we get together, we can pull out the stops!

We'll soon learn how to care for the land,
The sea, and the air — let's all lend a hand!

Please join our picnic. Come sing and cheer!
There's plenty to eat for everyone here!

Index

3456789 BP Printed in Canada 5432109